Jumpstarters for Pre-Algebra

Short Daily Warm-ups for the Classroom

By
CINDY BARDEN

COPYRIGHT © 2005 Mark Twain Media, Inc.

ISBN 10-digit: 1-58037-303-8
      13-digit: 978-1-58037-303-6

Printing No. CD-404030

Mark Twain Media, Inc., Publishers
Distributed by Carson-Dellosa Publishing Company, Inc.

The purchase of this book entitles the buyer to reproduce the student pages for classroom use only. Other permissions may be obtained by writing Mark Twain Media, Inc., Publishers.

All rights reserved. Printed in the United States of America.

Table of Contents

Introduction to Parents and Teachers 1
Student Reference Page 2
Addition 3
Subtraction 6
Multiplication 8
Arrays 10
Division 11
Mixed Operations: Math Stories 13
Decimals and Fractions 14
Order of Operations 15
Positive and Negative Numbers 17
Exponents 19
Multi-Step Math Stories 20
Operations Signs 21
Mixed Operations 22
Describing Number Patterns 23
Drawing a Picture or Diagram to Find a Pattern 24
Using Tables to Find Patterns 25
Math Stories With Patterns 26
Values of Variables 27
Balancing Equations 28
Isolating Variables 30
Step-by-Step 32
Variables in Measurement 33
Variables in Formulas 34
Multi-Step Operations With Variables 36
Value of Variables Using Clues 38
Equations With Two Variables 39
Answer Keys 40

Introduction to Parents and Teachers

Physical warm-ups help athletes prepare for more strenuous types of activity. Mental warm-ups help students prepare for the day's lesson while reviewing what they have previously learned.

The short warm-up activities presented in this book provide teachers and parents with activities to help students practice and reinforce the skills they have already learned. They are encouraged to use a variety of problem-solving techniques including making lists, logical reasoning, using and drawing diagrams, and using tables to find patterns.

Each page contains five warm-ups—one for each day of the week. Used at the beginning of class, warm-ups help students focus on a pre-algebra related topic. Activities on the same page are progressively more challenging.

The warm-ups include addition, subtraction, multiplication, division, fractions, decimals, math stories, number sense, place value, geometry, algebra, measurement, and other activities. They can be used in any order to best meet your teaching needs.

Copy the Student Reference Page for each student as a handy, quick-reference tool or enlarge it and post it in your classroom.

Suggestions for using the activity pages:

- Make copies for each student and cut apart one page each week. Give students one warm-up activity each day at the beginning of class.

- Give each student a copy of the entire page to complete day-by-day. Students can keep the completed pages in a three-ring binder to use as a resource for review.

- Make transparencies of individual warm-ups and complete the activities as a group.

- Provide extra copies of warm-ups in your learning center for students to complete at random when they have spare time for review.

- Keep some warm-ups on hand to use as fill-ins when the class has a few extra minutes before lunch or dismissal.

 # Pre-Algebra Warm-ups: Student Reference Page

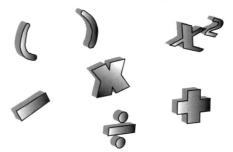

Order of Operations
Always solve equations in this order:
1. Perform operations inside parentheses.
2. Simplify exponents.
3. Multiply and divide from left to right.
4. Add and subtract from left to right.

Property of Equality
If you add, subtract, multiply, or divide both sides of a true equation by the same amount, the equation remains true.

Commutative Property of Addition
The sum of two or more numbers always remains the same, no matter the order in which they are added. *Examples:* 2 + 3 + 4 + 5 = 14 and 5 + 4 + 3 + 2 = 14

Commutative Property of Multiplication
The product of two or more numbers always remains the same, no matter the order in which they are multiplied. *Examples:* 2 x 3 x 4 = 24 and 4 x 2 x 3 = 24

Multiplication of Positive and Negative Numbers
When multiplying two or more positive numbers, the answer will always be a positive number. *Example:* 2 x 3 x 4 = 24

When multiplying a positive number by a negative number, the answer will always be a negative number. *Example:* -5 x 4 = -20

When multiplying a negative number by a negative number, the answer will always be a positive number. *Example:* -5 x -4 = 20

Division of Positive and Negative Numbers
When dividing a positive number by a positive number, the answer will always be a positive number. *Example:* 49 ÷ 7 = 7

When dividing a negative number by a negative number, the answer will always be a positive number. *Example:* -49 ÷ -7 = 7

When dividing a negative number by a positive number, the answer will always be a negative number. *Example:* -49 ÷ 7 = -7

When dividing a positive number by a negative number, the answer will always be a negative number. *Example:* 49 ÷ -7 = -7

Jumpstarters for Pre-Algebra   Addition

Pre-Algebra Warm-ups: Addition

Name/Date _____

Addition 1

Fill in the missing numbers to make the equations true.

A. 5 + _____ = 12   B. 4 + _____ = 16

C. 3 + _____ = 20   D. 7 + _____ = 18

Name/Date _____

Addition 2

Fill in the missing numbers to make the equations true.

A. _____ + 17 = 35   B. 21 + _____ = 47

C. _____ + 34 = 48   D. 11 + _____ = 50

Name/Date _____

Addition 3

A. If Josh has 42 quarters saved, how many more does he need to have 86 in all? _____

B. How many more pages will Dwight need to read to reach page 92, if he is on page 74 now? _____

C. Cheryl sold 61 boxes of candy. How many more will she need to sell to reach her last year's goal of 73? _____

D. What number added to 49 equals 91? _____

Name/Date _____

Addition 4

Fill in the missing numbers to make the equations true.

A. 6 + _____ + 4 = 19

B. 13 + _____ + 5 = 23

C. _____ + 8 + 4 = 32

D. 14 + 6 + _____ = 27

Name/Date _____

Addition 5

Fill in the missing numbers to make the equations true.

A. 4 + 9 = 6 + _____

B. _____ + 17 = 23 + 11

C. 8 + _____ = 12 + 15

D. 21 + 34 = _____ + 50

© Mark Twain Media, Inc., Publishers   3

Jumpstarters for Pre-Algebra   Addition

 # Pre-Algebra Warm-ups: Addition

Name/Date _____

Addition 6

Max found 17 seashells in the morning. He found more after lunch. Max found 32 seashells in all. Write an addition equation to show how many he found in the afternoon.

_____

Name/Date _____

Addition 7

The firefighters responded to 11 calls during the first two weeks in February. By the end of the month, they had responded to a total of 38 calls. How many calls did they respond to during the second two weeks of February?

_____

Name/Date _____

Addition 8

Will had 837 stamps in his collection. He had 187 stamps from Tobago. The rest of his stamps were from Fiji. How many stamps did Will have from Fiji?

_____

Name/Date _____

Addition 9

Phil had 18 football cards, 42 basketball cards, and 31 baseball cards. Jill had the same total number of cards. If she had 13 football cards and 28 basketball cards, how many baseball cards did she have?

_____

Name/Date _____

Addition 10

A. Raquel organized her baseball cap collection by color. She had 14 blue caps, 9 red caps, and 7 green caps. Then she sorted the caps by sports. She had 17 caps with pro team logos. The rest had college team logos. How many caps did Raquel have from college teams?

_____

B. Tomás lost 164 of his 416 broccoli seedlings to bug blight. The other seedlings grew so well that he had broccoli for dinner every night for a year. How many of his broccoli seedlings grew well?

_____

© Mark Twain Media, Inc., Publishers

Jumpstarters for Pre-Algebra   Addition

Pre-Algebra Warm-ups: Addition

Name/Date _____

Addition 11

Find the value of *n*.

A. $5 + n = 16$ B. $7 + n = 16$ C. $6 + n = 20$ D. $9 + n = 18$

    n = _____   n = _____   n = _____   n = _____

Name/Date _____

Addition 12

Find the value of *p*.

A. $p + \$17 = \$35$ B. $\$21 + p = \$47$

    p = _____   p = _____

C. $p + \$34 = \$48$ D. $\$11 + p = \$50$

    p = _____   p = _____

Name/Date _____

Addition 13

Write the value of *h*.

A. $0.42 + h = 0.86$ B. $h + 0.74 = 0.92$

    h = _____   h = _____

C. $0.61 + h = 0.73$ D. $h + 0.49 = 0.91$

    h = _____   h = _____

Name/Date _____

Addition 14

Find the value of *t*.

A. $7 + t + 4 = 19$ B. $12 + t + 5 = 23$

    t = _____   t = _____

C. $t + 8 + 4 = 31$ D. $14 + 6 + t = 25$

    t = _____   t = _____

Name/Date _____

Addition 15

Find the value of *g*.

A. $4 + 8 = 6 + g$ B. $g + 14 = 23 + 11$

    g = _____   g = _____

C. $7 + g = 11 + 15$ D. $12 + 34 = g + 30$

    g = _____   g = _____

© Mark Twain Media, Inc., Publishers

Pre-Algebra Warm-ups: Subtraction

Name/Date _____

Subtraction 1

Fill in the missing numbers to make the equations true.

A. 15 – _____ = 12

B. 24 – _____ = 17

C. 23 – _____ = 19

D. 37 – _____ = 19

Name/Date _____

Subtraction 2

Fill in the missing numbers to make the equations true.

A. _____ – 17 = 35   B. 51 – _____ = 47

C. _____ – 34 = 48   D. 92 – _____ = 50

Name/Date _____

Subtraction 3

Fill in the missing numbers to make the equations true.

A. 82 – _____ = 63   B. _____ – 94 = 12

C. 91 – _____ = 43   D. _____ – 64 = 31

Name/Date _____

Subtraction 4

Fill in the missing numbers to make the equations true.

A. 26 – _____ – 4 = 19   B. 33 – _____ – 7 = 23

C. _____ – 8 – 4 = 12   D. 64 – 6 – _____ = 7

Name/Date _____

Subtraction 5

Fill in the missing numbers to make the equations true.

A. 14 – 9 = 16 – _____   B. _____ – 17 = 23 – 11

C. 18 – _____ = 22 – 15   D. 41 – 24 = _____ – 50

Pre-Algebra Warm-ups: Subtraction

Name/Date _____

Subtraction 6

Find the value of n.

A. $45 - n = 35$
  $n = $ _____

B. $27 - n = 16$
  $n = $ _____

C. $66 - n = 20$
  $n = $ _____

D. $91 - n = 18$
  $n = $ _____

Name/Date _____

Subtraction 7

Find the value of p.

A. $p - \$17 = \$35$
  $p = $ _____

B. $\$91 - p = \$47$
  $p = $ _____

C. $p - \$34 = \$48$
  $p = $ _____

D. $\$89 - p = \$50$
  $p = $ _____

Name/Date _____

Subtraction 8

Write the value of h.

A. $h - 0.42 = 0.87$
  $h = $ _____

B. $h - 0.74 = 0.92$
  $h = $ _____

C. $0.61 - h = 0.33$
  $h = $ _____

D. $h - 0.49 = 0.91$
  $h = $ _____

Name/Date _____

Subtraction 9

Find the value of t.

A. $7 - t + 14 = 19$
  $t = $ _____

B. $12 - t + 25 = 23$
  $t = $ _____

C. $t - 8 - 4 = 31$
  $t = $ _____

D. $74 - 6 - t = 25$
  $t = $ _____

Name/Date _____

Subtraction 10

Find the value of g.

A. $4 + 8 = 16 - g$
  $g = $ _____

B. $g - 14 = 23 - 11$
  $g = $ _____

C. $47 - g = 11 + 15$
  $g = $ _____

D. $12 + 34 = g - 30$
  $g = $ _____

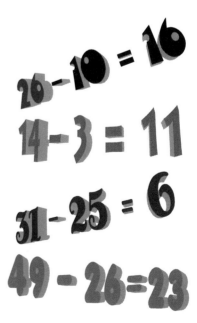

Pre-Algebra Warm-ups: Multiplication

Name/Date _____

Multiplication 1

Fill in the missing numbers to make the equations true.

A. How many groups of 7 are needed to equal 70? _____

B. Bob put his 63 books into 21 stacks. How many books were in each stack? _____

C. Shelly had 48 stuffed animals. She arranged them by type and had 12 of each type. How many types did she have? _____

D. What number times 11 = 99? _____

Name/Date _____

Multiplication 2

Fill in the missing numbers to make the equations true.

A. 5 ____ = 20   B. 4 ____ = 16

C. 3 ____ = 21   D. 7 ____ = 28

Name/Date _____

Multiplication 3

Fill in the missing numbers to make the equations true.

A. 3 5 ____ = 30

B. ____ 7 2 = 56

C. 4 ____ 3 = 36

D. ____ 4 9 = 108

Name/Date _____

Multiplication 4

Fill in the missing numbers to make the equations true.

A. 6 ____ 4 = 48

B. 3 ____ 5 = 45

C. ____ 8 4 = 32

D. 4 7 ____ = 56

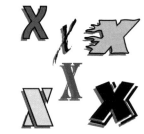

Name/Date _____

Multiplication 5

Fill in the missing numbers to make the equations true.

A. 4 9 = 3 ____

B. ____ 7 = 21 2

C. 8 ____ = 6 4

D. 4 13 = ____ 2

Pre-Algebra Warm-ups: Multiplication

Name/Date _____

Multiplication 6

Find the value of m.

A. 5 · m = 25

m = _____

B. 4 · m = 16

m = _____

C. m · 3 = 21

m = _____

D. m · 7 = 42

m = _____

Name/Date _____

Multiplication 7

Find the value of p.

A. 25 · p = 100

p = _____

B. 41 · p = 123

p = _____

C. 15 · p = 105

p = _____

D. p · 4 = 24

p = _____

Name/Date _____

Multiplication 8

Write the value of k.

A. 3 · 5 · k = 30

k = _____

B. k · 7 · 2 = 56

k = _____

C. 4 · k · 3 = 36

k = _____

D. k · 4 · 9 = 108

k = _____

Name/Date _____

Multiplication 9

Find the value of s.

A. s^2 = 100

s = _____

B. 40 · s = 160

s = _____

C. 11 · s = 99

s = _____

D. 8 · s = 56

s = _____

Name/Date _____

Multiplication 10

A. Stacy gave each of her 21 classmates the same number of markers. In all, she gave out 147 markers. How many markers did she give to each classmate?

_____

B. Tobias spent the same amount of money for holiday gifts for 8 friends. He spent $72 in all. How much did he spend on each gift?

_____

Jumpstarters for Pre-Algebra   Arrays

 # Pre-Algebra Warm-ups: Arrays

Name/Date _____

Arrays 1

An array shows objects in columns and rows. Each row has the same number of objects. Each column has the same number of objects.

Write two multiplication sentences for this array:

* * * * * * * * * *   _____
* * * * * * * * * *
* * * * * * * * * *   _____

Name/Date _____

Arrays 2

On your own paper, draw an array to show each fact. Then find the product.

A. 3   5 = _____
B. 4   9 = _____
C. 2   12 = _____
D. 1   15 = _____

Name/Date _____

Arrays 3

Write two multiplication sentences for each array.

A. ♦ ♦ ♦ ♦ ♦ ♦ ♦ ♦
    ♦ ♦ ♦ ♦ ♦ ♦ ♦ ♦
    ♦ ♦ ♦ ♦ ♦ ♦ ♦ ♦
    ♦ ♦ ♦ ♦ ♦ ♦ ♦ ♦

_____

_____

B. ♥ ♥ ♥ ♥ ♥ ♥ ♥
    ♥ ♥ ♥ ♥ ♥ ♥ ♥
    ♥ ♥ ♥ ♥ ♥ ♥ ♥
    ♥ ♥ ♥ ♥ ♥ ♥ ♥
    ♥ ♥ ♥ ♥ ♥ ♥ ♥

_____

_____

Name/Date _____

Arrays 4

A. Kasey bought a package of stickers. Each page had 3 rows of stickers with 9 stickers in each row. There were 5 pages in the package. How many stickers were in the package? _____

B. Trixie planted 8 rows of turnips in her garden. She planted 24 turnips in each row. How many turnips did she plant? _____

Name/Date _____

Arrays 5

On your own paper, draw an array to show the math story. Solve.

Mel sewed 12 buttons on each strip of cloth and sewed 13 strips of cloth together to make a large rectangle. How many buttons did Mel sew in all?

_____

© Mark Twain Media, Inc., Publishers   10

Jumpstarters for Pre-Algebra — Division

 # Pre-Algebra Warm-ups: Division

Name/Date _____

Division 1

Fill in the missing numbers to make the equations true.

A. 36 ÷ _____ = 6 B. _____ ÷ 8 = 6

C. 99 ÷ _____ = 9 D. _____ ÷ 7 = 5

Name/Date _____

Division 2

Fill in the missing numbers to make the equations true.

A. $44 ÷ _____ = $11 B. _____ ÷ 14 = $2

C. $72 ÷ _____ = $9 D. _____ ÷ 12 = $12

Name/Date _____

Division 3

Fill in the missing numbers to make the equations true.

A. 46 ÷ _____ = 7 R4 B. _____ ÷ 8 = 7 R6

C. 84 ÷ _____ = 9 R3 D. _____ ÷ 11 = 5 R10

Name/Date _____

Division 4

Fill in the missing numbers to make the equations true.

A. 1,000 ÷ _____ = 100 B. _____ ÷ 5 = 40

C. 10,000 ÷ _____ = 100 D. _____ ÷ 30 = 1,500

Name/Date _____

Division 5

A. Jeanna placed her frog statues on four shelves. She put 23 on each shelf. Write a division equation to show how many frog statues she had.

_____

B. Alvin jogged every day for a week. He covered 56 miles. Write a division equation to show how far he ran if he ran the same number of miles each day.

_____

Jumpstarters for Pre-Algebra · Division

 # Pre-Algebra Warm-ups: Division

Name/Date _____

Division 6

Find the value of w.

A. $36 \div w = 6$

w = _____

B. $w \div 8 = 6$

w = _____

C. $99 \div w = 9$

w = _____

D. $w \div 7 = 5$

w = _____

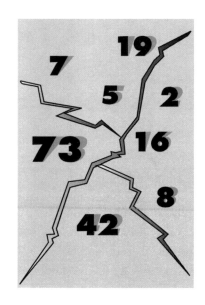

Name/Date _____

Division 7

Find the value of v.

A. $\$55 \div v = \$11$

v = _____

B. $v \div 14 = \$3$

v = _____

C. $\$81 \div v = \$9$

v = _____

D. $v \div 12 = \$11$

v = _____

Name/Date _____

Division 8

Find the value of r.

A. $45 \div r = 7\ R3$

r = _____

B. $r \div 8 = 7\ R2$

r = _____

C. $86 \div r = 9\ R5$

r = _____

D. $r \div 11 = 5\ R9$

r = _____

Name/Date _____

Division 9

Find the value of h.

A. $1{,}000 \div h = 100$

h = _____

B. $h \div 5 = 20$

h = _____

C. $100{,}000 \div h = 100$

h = _____

D. $h \div 30 = 2{,}100$

h = _____

Name/Date _____

Division 10

A. What number divided by 7 equals the sum of 3 and 5?

_____

B. What number divided by the sum of 8 and 4 equals 5?

_____

© Mark Twain Media, Inc., Publishers   12

Pre-Algebra Warm-ups: Mixed Operations: Math Stories

Name/Date _____

Mixed Operations: Math Stories 1

Grandma baked cookies. She gave 7 to Sandy. She gave half of what were left, plus one, to Sue. She gave 3 to Stan. Then she gave half of what were left to Steve. Since there were only two cookies left, she ate them herself.

How many cookies did she bake? _____

Name/Date _____

Mixed Operations: Math Stories 2

A. In a game, each player receives the same amount of play money. They each get twenty-five $1's, three $5's, four $10's, two $100's. How much money does each player get? _____

B. Jacob had 7 dimes, 14 nickels, 3 quarters, and 2 half-dollars. How much did he have in all? _____

Name/Date _____

Mixed Operations: Math Stories 3

A. Roberto has 12 books to stack. List six ways he could stack them so there are an equal number of books in each stack.

_____   _____

_____   _____

_____   _____

B. Carol has a piece of cloth that is 7 inches long and 25 inches wide. How many 5- by 7-inch rectangles can she cut from it? _____

Name/Date _____

Mixed Operations: Math Stories 4

A. Gina has $33 in bills. She has more than one $10 bill. She has more ones than tens. How many ones does she have? _____

B. Mario has less than $50. He has six bills in all. Four of them are tens. He has fewer ones than tens. How many ones does he have? _____

Name/Date _____

Mixed Operations: Math Stories 5

A. Juan has fewer than ten $10 bills. He has more than three $1 bills. He has twice as many tens as ones. How much money does he have? _____

B. At a farmer's market, carrots are on sale, three bunches for $1. Each bunch contains five carrots. How many carrots would you get for $3? _____

Pre-Algebra: Warm-Ups Decimals and Fractions

Name/Date _____

Decimals and Fractions 1

Write the decimals as fractions. Reduce to lowest terms.

A. 0.75 = _____   B. 0.95 = _____   C. 0.2 = _____

D. 0.34 = _____   E. 0.01 = _____   F. 7.14 = _____

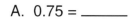

Name/Date _____

Decimals and Fractions 2

Write the fractions as decimals.

A. $\frac{4}{5}$ = _____   B. $\frac{9}{10}$ = _____

C. $\frac{7}{100}$ = _____   D. $\frac{7}{8}$ = _____

E. $\frac{2}{4}$ = _____   F. $5\frac{3}{5}$ = _____

Name/Date _____

Decimals and Fractions 3

Fill in the missing numbers to make the equations true. Reduce fractions to lowest terms.

A. $9\frac{1}{2} + 7\frac{3}{4}$ = _____   B. $3\frac{5}{8} - 2\frac{9}{10}$ = _____

C. $\frac{2}{3} \div \frac{9}{16}$ = _____   D. $\frac{4}{7}\ \frac{5}{8}$ = _____

Name/Date _____

Decimals and Fractions 4

Fill in the missing numbers to make the equations true.

A. $\frac{3}{4}$ + _____ = $1\frac{1}{4}$

B. 0.3 _____ = 0.9

C. 0.42 – _____ = 0.24

D. _____ ÷ $\frac{1}{2}$ = 10

Name/Date _____

Decimals and Fractions 5

Fill in the missing numbers to make the equations true.

A. $\frac{1}{2}$ + _____ = 0.5 + 0.75

B. 0.8 _____ = 1.2 + 2

C. $1\frac{3}{4}$ + _____ = 32

D. 7 + _____ = 0.6 + 9

Jumpstarters for Pre-Algebra									Order of Operations

Pre-Algebra: Warm-ups
Order of Operations

Name/Date _____

Order of Operations 1

Review the order of operations steps. Solve the equations.

A. 3   5 + 7 = _____

B. 6 + 2   4 = _____

C. 5 + 3   2 + 4 = _____

D. 11 + 7 + 4   8 = _____

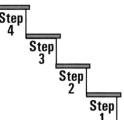

Name/Date _____

Order of Operations 2

Review the order of operations steps. Solve the equations.

A. 5   7 − 4 = _____

B. 11   4 − 9 = _____

C. 8 − 3   9 − 6 = _____

D. 13 − 5 − 2   13 = _____

Name/Date _____

Order of Operations 3

Review the order of operations steps. Solve the equations.

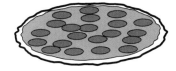

A. Jack ordered 6 pizzas for his party at $14 each. He used a $5 off the total coupon. What was his total?

   _____

B. Maisie received $4 per hour for babysitting. The Andersons paid her for 3 hours and gave her an additional $6. How much did she receive in all?

   _____

Name/Date _____

Order of Operations 4

Review the order of operations steps. Solve the equations.

A. (6 + 2)   (3 + 4) = _____

B. (37 − 2) ÷ 7 = _____

C. (9 ÷ 3)   (2   4) = _____

D. (0.7   0.2) − (0.5 + 0.3) = _____

Name/Date _____

Order of Operations 5

Review the order of operations steps. Solve the equations.

A. 10^2 + 2 = _____

B. (6   3) ÷ (9 − 6) = _____

C. 3 3^2 − 1 = _____

D. (10 ÷ 2) + (24 − 12)   (3 + 6) = _____

© Mark Twain Media, Inc., Publishers

Jumpstarters for Pre-Algebra   Order of Operations

Pre-Algebra Warm-ups: Order of Operations

Name/Date _____

Order of Operations 6

Fill in the missing numbers to make the equations true.

A. 6(_____ + 2) – (4   5) = 40

B. 3(_____ + 3) + 2 = 23

C. (23 – _____) ÷ 2 = 10

Name/Date _____

Order of Operations 7

Fill in the missing numbers to make the equations true.

A. (_____   3) + (4   6) = 30

B. 48 ÷ (12 – _____) = 8

C. 8 + (36 ÷ _____) + 1 = 13

Name/Date _____

Order of Operations 8

Fill in the missing numbers to make the equations true.

A. (11 + _____) ÷ 4 = 4

B. (6   3 + _____) ÷ 2 = 14

C. (14 + 14) ÷ _____ = 7

Name/Date _____

Order of Operations 9

Fill in the missing numbers to make the equations true.

A. 4 + (_____   _____) = 10

B. 3   (_____ – _____) = 3

C. (4   _____) + _____ = 31

Name/Date _____

Order of Operations 10

Fill in the missing numbers to make the equations true.

A. (6   4) + (_____   5) = 64   B. 3   (9 – _____) = 0

C. 4² (_____ – 6) = 64   D. (3   7) + _____ = 21

8 + (10 × __) = 38

(5 – 2) + ___ = 21

3² × (__ – 4) = 18

Pre-Algebra Warm-ups: Positive and Negative Numbers

Name/Date _____

Positive and Negative Numbers 1

A. The temperature started at -8°.
   It increased 19°.
   The temperature is now _____.

B. The temperature started at 28°.
   It decreased 19°.
   The temperature is now _____.

Name/Date _____

Positive and Negative Numbers 2

A. The temperature started at -32°.
   It increased 9°.
   The temperature is now _____.

B. The temperature started at -17°.
   It decreased 29°.
   The temperature is now _____.

Name/Date _____

Positive and Negative Numbers 3

A. The temperature started at -6°.
   It increased 36°.
   The temperature is now _____.

B. Between 6 A.M. and noon, the temperature increased 35°, to a high of 14°. What was the temperature at 6 A.M.? _____

Name/Date _____

Positive and Negative Numbers 4

Cassie owed her brother $17.50. She borrowed another $13.25 from her sister and $7.75 from her best friend. She used $20 she received for her birthday to pay part of her debt. How much does she still owe?

_____

Name/Date _____

Positive and Negative Numbers 5

Fill in the chart to show how much Karl owed after paying $120 over 6 months on a $400 item he charged. Use a calculator. To find the amount of monthly interest, multiply the balance by 0.2, and then divide by 12. Round to the nearest cent.

Amount Due	Amount Paid	Balance	20% Interest	New Balance
$400.00	$20.00	$380.00	$6.33	$386.33
$386.33	$20.00	$366.33	_____	_____
_____	$20.00	_____	_____	_____
_____	$20.00	_____	_____	_____
_____	$20.00	_____	_____	_____
_____	$20.00	_____	_____	_____

Jumpstarters for Pre-Algebra Positive and Negative Numbers

Pre-Algebra Warm-ups: Positive and Negative Numbers

Name/Date _____

Positive and Negative Numbers 6

Use each of these numbers only once in each equation to make each equation true:
-1, -3, and -5.

A. ____ + ____ + ____ = -9

B. (____ ____) + ____ = +2

C. (____ ____) + ____ = +14

D. (____ + ____) ÷ ____ = +8

Name/Date _____

Positive and Negative Numbers 7

Use each of these numbers only once in each equation to make each equation true:
-2, -4, and -6.

A. (____ + ____) ÷ ____ = +2

B. (____ ____) + ____ = +22

C. (____ ____) + ____ = +2

D. ____ + ____ + ____ = -12

Name/Date _____

Positive and Negative Numbers 8

Use each of these numbers only once in each equation to make each equation true:
-5, -6, and -7.

A. ____ + ____ + ____ = -18

B. (____ ____) + ____ = +37

C. (____ ____) + ____ = +23

D. (____ ____) ÷ ____ = 4 R2

Name/Date _____

Positive and Negative Numbers 9

Use each of these numbers only once in each equation to make each equation true:
-1, -3, and -5.

A. (____ + ____) ____ = +20

B. ____ + (____ ÷ ____) = +2

C. (____ + ____) ____ = +18

D. (____ ____) ÷ ____ = -15

Name/Date _____

Positive and Negative Numbers 10

Use each of these numbers only once in each equation to make each equation true:
-4, -5, -6.

A. (____ ____) ÷ ____ = -7 R2

B. (____ ____) ÷ ____ = -4 R4

C. ____ + ____ + ____ = -15

D. ____ (____ + ____) = +54

Pre-Algebra Warm-ups: Exponents

Name/Date _____

Exponents 1

2^2 contains an exponent. It means the same as 2 · 2. The value of $2^2 = 4$.

2^3 contains an exponent. It means the same as 2 · 2 · 2. The value of $2^3 = 8$.

A. 2^4 means the same as _____.

B. 9^6 means the same as _____.

C. 7^3 means the same as _____.

D. y^{10} means the same as _____.

Name/Date _____

Exponents 2

Find the value of each exponential expression.

A. 3^3 _____

B. 4^2 _____

C. 2^5 _____

D. 5^3 _____

Name/Date _____

Exponents 3

Write the exponential expression for each multiplication expression.

A. 3 · 3 · 3 = _____

B. 10 · 10 · 10 · 10 · 10 · 10 = _____

C. $d \cdot d \cdot d$ = _____

D. $m \cdot m + p \cdot p$ = _____

Name/Date _____

Exponents 4

Solve the equations.

A. $7 + 3^2 =$ _____

B. $42 - 4^2 =$ _____

C. $3^3 - 3 =$ _____

D. $9^2 - 48 =$ _____

Name/Date _____

Exponents 5

Write the exponential expressions that equal the amounts given.

A. 36 = _____   B. 81 = _____

C. 16 = _____   D. 25 = _____

Pre-Algebra Warm-ups: Multi-Step Math Stories

Multi-Step Math Stories 1

A. The Lovely Lawn Landscaping Company charges $8 per square foot to lay sod. Mr. Berenz needs new sod in an area 40 feet by 30 feet. How much will it cost him to have new sod laid? _____

B. The Lovely Lawn Landscaping Company charges 5¢ a pound for decorative rock, plus a $25 delivery fee. How much will it cost to have 3 tons of rock delivered? _____

Multi-Step Math Stories 2

Mr. Mikkelson's six children bought their dad a new electric saw for Father's Day. His youngest daughter could only afford to contribute $20. The other five divided the rest of the cost equally among them. If the saw cost $170, how much did it cost each of the other children?

_____

Multi-Step Math Stories 3

A. Devin spends the same amount for lunch each day, Monday through Friday. On Saturday and Sunday, he spends $3 a day more. Circle the algebraic expression that represents how much Devin spends in one week.

1. $7d$ 2. $5d + 2(d+3)$ 3. $5d + 2d$

B. Jesse and Jim each paid half the cost of a new DVD player. In addition, Jesse paid the 5% sales tax. Circle the algebraic expression that represents how much Jesse paid.

1. $c \; 5\% + \frac{1}{2}c$ 2. $\frac{1}{2}c + 5\%$ 3. $\frac{1}{2}c + \frac{1}{2}c = 5\%$

Multi-Step Math Stories 4

A. Devin spends $4 a day for lunch each day, Monday through Friday. On Saturday and Sunday he spends $3 more a day. How much does he spend for lunch in a six-week period? _____

B. Jesse and Jim each paid half the cost of a $150 DVD player. In addition, Jesse paid the 5% sales tax. How much did Jesse pay? _____

Multi-Step Math Stories 5

On another sheet of paper, write a multi-step math story with variables. Trade papers with a partner and solve.

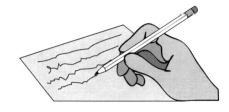

Jumpstarters for Pre-Algebra

 # Pre-Algebra Warm-ups: Operations Signs

Name/Date _____

Operations Signs 1

Balance the equations by filling in the missing operations signs.

A. 17 ___ 14 = 31
B. 81 ___ 9 = 9
C. 17 ___ 4 = 68
D. 5,286 ___ 3,541 = 1,745

Name/Date _____

Operations Signs 2

Balance the equations by filling in the missing operations signs.

A. n ___ 6 = 6n
B. 12 ___ n = n + 12
C. 16 ___ n = 10 + 4
D. n + 14 = 7 + 7 ___ n

Name/Date _____

Operations Signs 3

Balance the equations by filling in the missing operations signs.

A. $\frac{1}{2}$ ___ $\frac{1}{2}$ = 1
B. $\frac{3}{4}$ ___ $\frac{1}{2}$ = $1\frac{1}{2}$
C. $\frac{1}{2}$ ___ $\frac{1}{2}$ = $\frac{1}{4}$
D. $\frac{1}{2}$ ___ $\frac{1}{2}$ ___ 2 = 3

Name/Date _____

Operations Signs 4

Write <, >, or = to make the number sentences true.

A. 17 ___ 2   7
B. n ___ n + 8
C. n – 9 ___ n – 11
D. n + 14 ___ n + 7 + 7

Name/Date _____

Operations Signs 5

Write <, >, ≤, ≥, or = to make the number sentences true.

A. $m + n + y + z$ ___ $n + m + z + y$
B. $t + u$ ___ $t - u$
C. $7v + 8v - 11v$ ___ $8v - 11v + 7v$
D. 6   4 ___ $n + 2$, if $n = 9$
E. $16t$ ___ $16 + t$, if $t > 1$
F. $16t \div 2$ ___ $16t$ 2

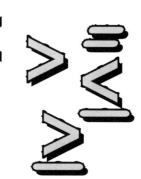

© Mark Twain Media, Inc., Publishers

Jumpstarters for Pre-Algebra   Mixed Operations

 # Pre-Algebra Warm-ups: Mixed Operations

Name/Date _____

Mixed Operations 1

Work clockwise, starting at the top of the figure. Fill in the missing number. Your starting number is also your ending number.

   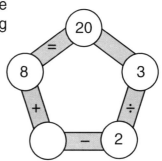

Name/Date _____   Name/Date _____

Mixed Operations 2   ## Mixed Operations 3

Work clockwise, starting at the top of the figure. Fill in the missing number. Your starting number is also your ending number.   Work clockwise, starting at the top of the figure. Fill in the missing number. Your starting number is also your ending number.

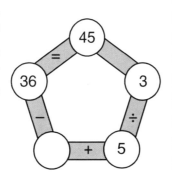   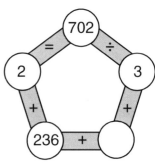

Name/Date _____   Name/Date _____

Mixed Operations 4   ## Mixed Operations 5

Work clockwise, starting at the top of the figure. Fill in the missing operations signs. Your starting number is also your ending number.   Work clockwise, starting at the top of the figure. Fill in the missing number. Your starting number is also your ending number.

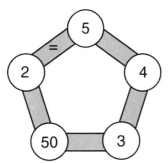   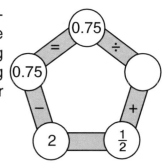

© Mark Twain Media, Inc., Publishers

Pre-Algebra Warm-ups: Describing Number Patterns

Name/Date _____

Describing Number Patterns 1

Find the pattern.

Example: 1, 2, 3, ___, 5, 6

The missing number is 4.

The algebraic expression for the pattern rule is $n + 1$.

Find the pattern. Fill in the missing number. Describe the pattern rule using an algebraic expression.

7, 14, 21, 28, ___, 42, 49

Algebraic expression: _____

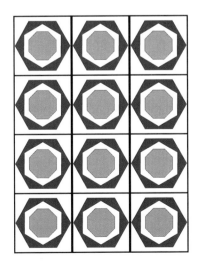

Name/Date _____

Describing Number Patterns 2

Find the pattern. Fill in the missing numbers. Describe the pattern rule.

A. 2, 4, 8, 16, ___, 64, ___
   Algebraic expression: _____

B. 99, 88, ___, ___, ___, ___, 33
   Algebraic expression: _____

Name/Date _____

Describing Number Patterns 3

Find the pattern. Fill in the missing numbers. Describe the pattern rule.

A. 3, 7, 15, ___, 63, 127
   Algebraic expression: _____

B. 128, 64, 32, ___, 8, 4
   Algebraic expression: _____

Name/Date _____

Describing Number Patterns 4

Write an algebraic expression to describe the pattern.

One cat has two ears. Two cats have four ears. How many ears do an unknown number of cats have?

Algebraic expression: _____

Name/Date _____

Describing Number Patterns 5

Write an algebraic expression to describe the pattern.

Jason jogged three miles on Sunday, and then jogged two more miles each day for a week.

Algebraic expression: _____

Pre-Algebra Warm-ups: Drawing a Picture or Diagram to Find a Pattern

Name/Date _____

Drawing a Picture or Diagram 1

Drawing a picture or diagram can help you find patterns. Your drawings do not need to be detailed. You can use simple circles, X's, or squares to represent items.

A mother duck led a large group of ducklings. There were two ducklings in the row behind her, and three ducklings in the row following them. All the ducklings followed the same pattern. There were five rows of ducklings.

On your own paper, draw a picture or diagram to represent the ducklings.

How many ducklings were there in all? _____

Name/Date _____

Drawing a Picture or Diagram 2

George stacked cans of tomato juice for a grocery store display. When he finished, there was one can on the top, two cans in the second layer from the top, and six cans in the fourth layer from the top. On your own paper, draw a picture to show the story.

If he stacked all cans in this pattern and the stack was six layers high, how many cans were in the bottom layer? _____

Name/Date _____

Drawing a Picture or Diagram 3

On your own paper, draw the next set of diamonds in this pattern.

♦   ♦ ♦   ♦ ♦ ♦   ♦ ♦ ♦ ♦
         ♦ ♦   ♦ ♦ ♦   ♦ ♦ ♦ ♦
                    ♦ ♦ ♦   ♦ ♦ ♦ ♦
                                 ♦ ♦ ♦ ♦

Name/Date _____

Drawing a Picture or Diagram 4

On your own paper, draw the next two sets of apples in this pattern.

Name/Date _____

Drawing a Picture or Diagram 5

On your own paper, draw a pattern of items for this algebraic expression: $n + 3$. Start with three items.

Pre-Algebra Warm-ups: Using Tables to Find Patterns

Name/Date _____

Using Tables to Find Patterns 1

One cold January day, the temperature started dropping at 3 P.M. It dropped two degrees each hour until 10 P.M. Fill in the table. If it was 3° at 3 P.M., what was the temperature at 10 P.M.?

Time	3 P.M.	4 P.M.	5 P.M.	6 P.M.	7 P.M.	8 P.M.	9 P.M.	10 P.M.
Temperature	3°	1°	___	___	___	___	___	___

Name/Date _____

Using Tables to Find Patterns 2

Everett had 35 red and white balloons. He had two red ones for every three white ones. Fill in the table to find how many red ones he had. How many were red?

red	2	4	___	___	___	___	___
white	3	6	___	___	___	___	___
total	5	10	___	___	___	___	___

Name/Date _____

Using Tables to Find Patterns 3

The "red eye" express can hold 56 passengers. Last night it had one empty seat for each six passengers. Fill in the table. How many people rode the "red eye" last night?

passengers	6	___	___	___	___	___	___
empty seats	1	___	___	___	___	___	___
total seats		___	___	___	___	___	___

Name/Date _____

Using Tables to Find Patterns 4

Jenny spent 10 hours last week reading and playing computer games. She played computer games 45 minutes for each 30 minutes she spent reading. Fill in the table. How much time did she spend reading last week?

reading	30	___	___	___	___	___	___
games	45	___	___	___	___	___	___
total time		___	___	___	___	___	___

Name/Date _____

Using Tables to Find Patterns 5

Grace has 77 CDs in her music collection of rock, country, and jazz music. She has twice as many rock CDs as jazz. She has two country CDs for each three jazz CDs. Make a table on another sheet of paper.

How many of each type does she have?

Rock _____

Country _____

Jazz _____

Pre-Algebra Warm-ups: Math Stories With Patterns

Math Stories With Patterns 1

Sasha scored 52% on her first math test. She increased her score by 4% on each of the next 11 tests.

A. What was her score on test number 6? _____

B. What was her score on test number 12? _____

Math Stories With Patterns 2

Robin spent 10 minutes reading her book the first day. She increased her reading time by 12 minutes each day.

A. How many minutes a day did she read on the third day? _____

B. How many minutes a day did she read on the ninth day? _____

Math Stories With Patterns 3

A DVD at DVD Discounts was originally priced at $20. It went on sale at 10% off. Each week it did not sell, the price was reduced by an additional 10% of the previous cost.

A. What was its sale price in week four? _____

B. What was the sale price in week six? _____

Math Stories With Patterns 4

Kisha made 126 errors on the first draft of her research paper. She decreased the number of errors by 21 each time she proofread her work. How many times will she need to proofread her work to reduce the number of errors to zero?

_____

Math Stories With Patterns 5

At a pedigreed dog show parade, a member of the audience counted 22 heads and 72 legs in the arena at one time. How many dogs and how many owners were in the parade?

_____

Pre-Algebra Warm-ups: Values of Variables

Name/Date _____

Values of Variables 1

Find the value of the expression $47 + n$ when:

A. $n = 5$ B. $n = 13$

_____   _____

C. $n = 6$ D. $n = 52$

_____   _____

Name/Date _____

Values of Variables 2

Find the value of the expression $71 - p$ when:

A. $p = 14$ B. $p = 71$

_____   _____

C. $p = 84$ D. $p = 11$

_____   _____

Name/Date _____

Values of Variables 3

Find the value of the expression $40 - (m \quad 4)$ when:

A. $m = 20$ B. $m = 7$

_____   _____

C. $m = 31$ D. $m = 19$

_____   _____

Name/Date _____

Values of Variables 4

A. A florist pays Mona 75¢ a bunch for dried lavender. Write an expression to show how much the florist will pay Mona for an unknown quantity of lavender. Let b equal the number of bunches Mona will sell.

_____

B. If Mona brings in 17 bunches of lavender, how much will the florist pay her?

_____

Name/Date _____

Values of Variables 5

A. A video store charges a late fee of $0.75 per item, plus $2 per day for videos or DVDs not returned on time. Write an expression to show how the fine is calculated. Let d equal the number of overdue days and m equal the number of items.

_____

B. If a DVD were eight days late, what would be the total late charges?

_____

Pre-Algebra Warm-ups: Balancing Equations

Name/Date _____

Balancing Equations 1

If the same amount is added to both sides of a true equation, the equation remains true.

Example: $3 + 4 = 7$ is a true equation. If 5 is added to both sides, the new equation is also true: $3 + 4 + 5 = 7 + 5$

Fill in the blanks to make the equations true.

A. $4 + 6 = 10$ $4 + 6 +$ _____ $= 10 + 9$
B. $z + 3 = 6$ $z + 3 + 3 = 6 +$ _____
C. $17 - 11 = 6$ $17 - 11 + 12 =$ _____

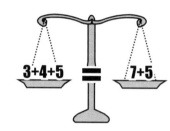

Name/Date _____

Balancing Equations 2

If the same amount is subtracted from both sides of a true equation, the equation remains true. Fill in the blanks to make the equations true.

A. $16 - 9 = 7$ $16 - 9 - 5 = 7 -$ _____
B. $4 \cdot 8 = 32$ $4 \cdot 8 -$ _____ $= 32 - 5$
C. $z + 9 = 31$ $z + 9 - 8 =$ _____

Name/Date _____

Balancing Equations 3

If both sides of a true equation are multiplied by the same amount, the equation remains true. Fill in the blanks to make the equations true.

A. $11 + 4 = 44$
_____ $\cdot 11 + 4 =$ _____ $\cdot 44$
B. $z - 101 = 700$
$z - 101 \cdot 4 = 700$ _____
C. $z \cdot 3 \cdot 0.5 = 3$ _____ $= 6 \cdot 3$

Name/Date _____

Balancing Equations 4

If both sides of a true equation are divided by the same amount, the equation remains true. Fill in the blanks to make the equations true.

A. $49 - 7 = 42$ $49 - 7 \div 7 = 42 \div$ _____
B. $8 + 12 = 20$ $20 \div 4 = 8 + 12 \div$ _____
C. $100 \div 5 = 20$ $100 \div 5 \div 1 =$ _____

Name/Date _____

Balancing Equations 5

Fill in the blanks to make the equations true.

A. $y + z = 9$ $y + z - 4 =$ _____
B. $21 \cdot 4 =$ _____ $21 \cdot 4 - 9 =$ _____
C. $y \div 11 = 42$ _____ $= 42 \cdot 4$

Balancing Equations 6

For each equation, write *add, subtract, multiply,* or *divide* to show which operation you should do to balance the equation.

A. $17 + r = 9$ _____

B. $t + 71 = 4$ _____

C. $g - 42 = 36$ _____

D. $w - 18 = 437$ _____

Balancing Equations 7

For each equation, write *add, subtract, multiply,* or *divide* to show which operation you should do to balance the equation.

A. $s \div 42 = 462$ _____

B. $27 \quad u = 108$ _____

C. $83 = 925 - v$ _____

D. $e \div 9 = 42$ _____

Balancing Equations 8

When balancing equations, the best number to add, subtract, multiply, or divide both sides of the equation by is the number that will isolate the variable on one side of the equation.

Example: To isolate the variable in this equation: $p - 70 = 94$, the best number to add to both sides of the equation would be 70. Then $p - 70 + 70 = 94 + 70$. Simplify the equation: $p = 164$

A. To solve this equation, $b + 702 = 941$, what is the best number to subtract from both sides of the equation? _____

B. To solve this equation: $c \div \frac{1}{2} = \frac{7}{8}$, what is the best number to multiply both sides of the equation by? _____

Balancing Equations 9

For each equation, write *add, subtract, multiply,* or *divide* to show which operation you should do to balance the equation.

A. $\frac{1}{2} \quad u = \frac{3}{4}$ _____

B. $z \div 0.337 = 3.033$ _____

C. $d - \frac{7}{16} = \frac{1}{4}$ _____

D. $n + 4{,}326 = 5{,}325$ _____

Balancing Equations 10

A. To solve this equation, $j - 6{,}491 = 419$, what is the best number to add to both sides of the equation? _____

B. To solve this equation, $12 \quad k = 144$, what is the best number to divide by on both sides of the equation? _____

Pre-Algebra Warm-ups: Isolating Variables

Name/Date _____

Isolating Variables 1

To find the value of a variable, first isolate it on one side of an equation by adding, subtracting, multiplying, or dividing both sides of the equation by the same amount.

Example: To isolate the variable in this equation: $n + 7 = 9$, subtract 7 from both sides of the equation. $n + 7 - 7 = 9 - 7$.
Then solve. $n = 2$

Isolate the variables by subtracting the same amount from both sides of the equation. Show your work.

A. $b + 48 = 52$ $b =$ _____

B. $c + 17 = 91$ $c =$ _____

C. $d + 21 = 49$ $d =$ _____

Name/Date _____

Isolating Variables 2

Isolate the variables by adding the same amount to both sides of the equation. Show your work.

A. $e - 7 = 16$ B. $f - 9 = 83$ C. $12 - g = 6$

$e =$ _____ $f =$ _____ $g =$ _____

Name/Date _____

Isolating Variables 3

Isolate the variables by dividing both sides of the equation by the same amount. Show your work.

A. $3\ h = 9$ B. $4\ j = 16$ C. $k\ 3 = 15$

$h =$ _____ $j =$ _____ $k =$ _____

Name/Date _____

Isolating Variables 4

Isolate the variables by multiplying both sides of the equation by the same amount. Show your work.

A. $m \div 4 = 3$ B. $n \div 3 = 7$ C. $p \div 8 = 5$

$m =$ _____ $n =$ _____ $p =$ _____

Name/Date _____

Isolating Variables 5

Isolate the variables. Show your work.

A. $3 + 4 + r = 10$ B. $17 - s = 4 + 12$ C. $12\ t = 6\ 6$

$r =$ _____ $s =$ _____ $t =$ _____

Pre-Algebra Warm-ups: Isolating Variables

Isolating Variables 6

Find the value of the variable in each equation.

A. $76 - s = 48$
s = _____

B. $t - 438 = 291$
t = _____

C. $3^3 - b = 25$
b = _____

D. $r - 6^2 = 47$
r = _____

Isolating Variables 7

Find the value of the variable in each equation.

A. $22 \quad g = 110$
g = _____

B. $r \quad 71 = 497$
r = _____

C. $(7 \quad 4) + a = 211$
a = _____

D. $y \quad y = 64$
y = _____

Isolating Variables 8

Find the value of the variable in each equation.

A. $(17 - h) \div 13 = 1$
h = _____

B. $e \div 36 = 8$
e = _____

C. $a \div (13 + 2) = 3$
a = _____

D. $7 = t \div 9$
t = _____

Isolating Variables 9

Find the value of the variable in each equation.

A. $16 = r^2$
r = _____

B. $e \quad e = 5^2$
e = _____

C. $a = 6^3 + 1$
a = _____

D. $27 = d \quad d \quad d$
d = _____

Isolating Variables 10

Find the value of the variable in each equation.

A. Megan had an unknown number of photos. She divided them into 10 groups with 12 photos in each group. Let p equal the number of photos. Write and solve an equation to show how many photos she had.

_____

B. LeRoy cut a length of string into 30 pieces, all the same length. If each piece of string was 13 inches long, how long was the string before he cut it?

_____

C. If he cut that same string into 10 equal pieces instead, how long would each piece be?

_____

Pre-Algebra Warm-ups: Step-by-Step

Name/Date _____

Step-by-Step 1

The park manager needs $5,387 to pay the balance on some new playground equipment. He has only $1,582 left in the budget. How much more does he need?

Write an equation for the math story. Use n for the unknown number: _____

Isolate the variable. Rewrite the equation: _____

Solve: $n =$ _____

Name/Date _____

Step-by-Step 2

Bryce needs 128 more hits to tie the city's baseball team record of 374 hits. How many does he have so far?

Write an equation for the math story. Use h for the unknown number: _____

Isolate the variable. Rewrite the equation: _____

Solve: $h =$ _____

Name/Date _____

Step-by-Step 3

After spending $4.36 at the mall, Michelle had $3.92 left. How much did she have to start?

Write an equation for the math story. Use m for the unknown number: _____

Isolate the variable. Rewrite the equation: _____

Solve: $m =$ _____

Name/Date _____

Step-by-Step 4

Lisa's pizza had 48 pieces of pepperoni. Each of its eight slices had the same number of pepperoni. How many pieces of pepperoni were on each slice?

Write an equation for the math story. Use p for the unknown number: _____

Isolate the variable. Rewrite the equation: _____

Solve: $p =$ _____

Name/Date _____

Step-by-Step 5

Jamie had 7 DVDs. Janice had 9 DVDs. When they combined their DVDs with Jill's, the total was 19. How many DVDs did Jill have?

Write an equation for the math story. Use j for the unknown number: _____

Isolate the variable. Rewrite the equation: _____

Solve: $j =$ _____

Pre-Algebra Warm-ups: Variables in Measurement

Variables in Measurement 1

Write an algebraic expression to show each measurement.

Example: The number of inches in an unknown number of feet

Let f = the variable.

Algebraic expression:
    12 f (or 12f)

A. The number of feet in an unknown number of yards

   Let b = the variable.

   Algebraic expression:

   _____

B. The number of ounces in an unknown number of pounds.

   Let z = the variable.

   Algebraic expression:

   _____

Variables in Measurement 2

Write an algebraic expression to show each measurement.

A. The number of feet in an unknown number of miles

   Let c = the variable. Algebraic expression: _____

B. The number of yards in an unknown number of inches

   Let d = the variable. Algebraic expression: _____

Variables in Measurement 3

Write an algebraic expression to show each measurement.

A. The number of cups in an unknown number of pints:

   Let e = the variable. Algebraic expression: _____

B. The number of gallons in an unknown number of quarts

   Let f = the variable. Algebraic expression: _____

Variables in Measurement 4

Write an algebraic expression to show each measurement.

A. The number of seconds in an unknown number of minutes

   Let g = the variable. Algebraic expression: _____

B. The number of minutes in an unknown number of days

   Let h = the variable. Algebraic expression: _____

Variables in Measurement 5

Write an algebraic expression to show each measurement.

A. The number of days in an unknown number of weeks:

   Let j = the variable. Algebraic expression: _____

B. The number of weeks in an unknown number of days:

   Let k = the variable. Algebraic expression: _____

Pre-Algebra Warm-ups: Variables in Formulas

Name/Date _____

Variables in Formulas 1

Area of a rectangle = length times width. This can be written as $A = lw$. l and w are variables. Write the equation. Then find the area of each rectangle.

A. length = 5 feet, width = 7 feet
   Equation: _____ Area = _____

B. length = 9 mm, width = 11 mm
   Equation: _____ Area = _____

Name/Date _____

Variables in Formulas 2

Area of a triangle = $\frac{1}{2}$ base times height. ($A = \frac{1}{2}bh$) Write the equation. Then find the area of each triangle.

A. base = 6 feet, height = 7 feet
   Equation: _____ Area = _____

B. base = 10 inches, height = 9 inches
   Equation: _____ Area = _____

Name/Date _____

Variables in Formulas 3

Volume of a rectangular prism = length times width times height. ($V = lwh$) Write the equation. Then find the volume of each rectangular prism.

A. 9-inch cube
   Equation: _____ Volume = _____

B. length = 4 feet, width = 7 feet, height = 8 feet
   Equation: _____ Volume = _____

C. l = 4 mm, w = 8 mm, h = 7 mm
   Equation: _____ Volume = _____

D. l = 6 cm, w = 2 cm, h = 25 cm
   Equation: _____ Volume = _____

Name/Date _____

Variables in Formulas 4

A. $A = lw$ means the _____ of a rectangle equals its _____ times its _____.

B. $A = \frac{1}{2}bh$ means _____.

C. $V = lwh$ means _____.

Name/Date _____

Variables in Formulas 5

A. A garden measures 25 feet by 28 feet. What is its area? _____

B. What is the area of a 4-inch square? _____

C. What is the volume of a 7-inch cube? _____

© Mark Twain Media, Inc., Publishers

Jumpstarters for Pre-Algebra   Variables in Formulas

 # Pre-Algebra Warm-ups: Variables in Formulas

Name/Date _____

Variables in Formulas 6

To find the distance traveled (d), multiply the rate of speed (r) by the time traveled (t).
$d = r \cdot t$ $r = d \div t$ $t = d \div r$

A. How far will Jackie travel in 4 hours if she drives 55 miles per hour?
Write and solve the equation: _____

B. A train covered 123 miles in 3 hours. At what speed did the train travel?
Write and solve the equation: _____

C. A truck driver spent 3 hours going 12 miles during a snowstorm. What was her rate in miles per hour? Write and solve the equation: _____

Name/Date _____

Variables in Formulas 7

Complete the chart.

Distance	Rate	Time
A. 428 miles	_____	20 hours
B. _____	25 feet per minute	9 minutes
C. 100 yards	_____	20 seconds

Name/Date _____

Variables in Formulas 8

A. Write and solve an equation to show how long a person walked if he covered 18 miles at the rate of 2.5 miles per hour.
_____

B. Write and solve an equation to show how fast a plane flew if it covered 867 miles in 3 hours.
_____

Name/Date _____

Variables in Formulas 9

A. The three-toed sloth averages 7 feet per minute on land and 15 feet per minute in the trees. How far would a three-toed sloth travel on land in an hour? _____

B. A cheetah can sprint for short distances at 60 miles per hour. How long would it take a cheetah to cover one-quarter of a mile at that rate? _____

Name/Date _____

Variables in Formulas 10

Use a reference source to find a speed record. On your own paper, write a math story problem that uses the distance/rate/time formula. Write the equation and the answer.

© Mark Twain Media, Inc., Publishers   35

Pre-Algebra Warm-ups: Multi-Step Operations With Variables

Name/Date _____

Multi-Step Operations With Variables 1

The 30 students in an advanced science class were ages 11, 12, and 13. One-half of the members were 12. Twenty percent were 11. The rest were 13. How many students of each age were in the class?

_____ 11-year-olds   _____ 12-year-olds

_____ 13-year-olds

Name/Date _____

Multi-Step Operations With Variables 2

Ricardo worked at a pet store. They had 300 fish in several huge aquariums. Fifteen percent were clownfish. He counted 15 angelfish. The tanks included twice as many neon tetras as zebra fish. How many of each type were in the aquariums?

_____ clownfish   _____ angelfish

_____ neon tetras   _____ zebra fish

Name/Date _____

Multi-Step Operations With Variables 3

At a tree farm, workers planted spruce, pine, and cedar saplings. They planted half as many spruce as pine. They planted three cedar for every four pine. They planted 96 spruce trees.

A. How many trees did they plant in all? _____

B. How many cedar trees did they plant? _____

Name/Date _____

Multi-Step Operations With Variables 4

For each two feet the tortoise raced, the hare covered 58 feet. How far ahead was the hare by the time the tortoise ran 12 feet?

_____

Name/Date _____

Multi-Step Operations With Variables 5

A. Violet had a dozen and a half roses, 26 carnations, and 3 dozen daisies. She put 2 roses, 4 carnations, and 3 daisies in each bouquet. What was the maximum number of bouquets she could make using that combination of flowers?

_____

B. If she wanted to use up the rest of the flowers and put a dozen flowers in each bouquet in any combination, how many more full bouquets could she make?

_____

Pre-Algebra Warm-ups: Multi-Step Operations With Variables

Multi-Step Operations With Variables 6

Marcus has twice as many green hats as red hats. He has 4 times as many blue hats as red hats. Marcus has a dozen blue hats.

How many green hats does he have? _____

How many red hats does he have? _____

Multi-Step Operations With Variables 7

Paul rode his bike twice as far as Penny. Pam rode her bike one-third as far as Paul. Penny rode 15 miles.

How far did Paul ride? _____

How far did Pam ride? _____

Multi-Step Operations With Variables 8

Mona has 3 times as many pepper plants as tomato plants in her garden. She has 4 times more basil plants than tomato plants. She has between 50 and 60 plants in her garden.

How many of each type of plant does she have?

_____ pepper   _____ tomato   _____ basil

Multi-Step Operations With Variables 9

Robin and Lark saw the same number of birds on their field trip. Jay saw half as many birds as either Robin or Lark. In all, they saw 600 birds.

How many birds did each one see?

_____ Robin   _____ Lark   _____ Jay

Multi-Step Operations With Variables 10

An extra super large pizza has equal amounts of shrimp and pepperoni slices. It has 4 times as many pineapple chunks as shrimp. There are 120 pieces of topping in all.

How many shrimp? _____
How many pepperoni slices? _____
How many pineapple chunks? _____

Pre-Algebra Warm-ups: Value of Variables Using Clues

Name/Date _____

Value of Variables Using Clues

What is the lowest possible value of t if …

　　t is a multiple of 3, and
　　t is greater than 100, and
　　t is an odd number?

The lowest possible value of $t =$ _____.

Name/Date _____

Value of Variables Using Clues

What is the highest possible value of b if …
　　b is less than 150, and
　　b is divisible by 4, and
　　all digits are even?

The highest possible value of $b =$ _____.

Name/Date _____

Value of Variables Using Clues 3

What is the only possible value of w if …
　　w is a number between 46 and 56, and
　　w is an odd number, and
　　w is evenly divisible by 3?

The only possible value of $w =$ _____.

Name/Date _____

Value of Variables Using Clues 4

What are two possible values of n, if …
　　n is a multiple of 5, and n is divisible by 3, and
　　the number in the ones place is 5, and
　　n is less than 100?

Two possible values of $n =$ _____ and _____.

Name/Date _____

Value of Variables Using Clues 5

What is the value of c, if…
　　c is greater than $3(4 + 12)$, and
　　c is less than 50, and c is divisible by 7, and
　　c is an odd number?

The only possible value of $c =$ _____.

Pre-Algebra Warm-ups: Equations With Two Variables

Name/Date _____

Equations With Two Variables 1

Example: Find the value of y. Let $m = 4$. $m + y = 13$ $y = 9$

Find the value of y. Let $m = 8$.

A. $m + y = 43$ B. $y - m = 43$ C. $m\ y = 56$ D. $m \div y = 2$

$y =$ _____ $y =$ _____ $y =$ _____ $y =$ _____

Name/Date _____

Equations With Two Variables 2

Find the value of g. Let $h = \frac{1}{2}$

A. $h + g = 7\frac{3}{4}$ B. $g \div h = 14$

$g =$ _____ $g =$ _____

C. $h\ g = 1$ D. $g - h = 16\frac{3}{4}$

$g =$ _____ $g =$ _____

Name/Date _____

Equations With Two Variables 3

Solve the equations. Let $c = 4$. Let $d = 8$.

A. $c + d =$ _____

B. $d \div c =$ _____

C. $c\ d =$ _____

D. $d\ 4 + c \div 4 =$ _____

Name/Date _____

Equations With Two Variables 4

Write an algebraic expression for each math story. Use r and t for variables.

A. Todd had some science books. Rachel had some history books. Together, they had 73 books. _____

B. After Oscar lost some weight, he weighed 128 pounds. _____

Name/Date _____

Equations With Two Variables 5

Write an algebraic expression for each math story. Use v and w for variables.

A. Melissa divided all of her CDs among her brothers and sisters. Each person received 8 CDs. _____

B. Max organized his photos in an album. He put the same number of photos on each page. Max filled 84 pages. _____

Answer Keys

Teachers: Check students' work and equations if necessary.

Addition 1 (p. 3)
A. 7   B. 12   C. 17   D. 11

Addition 2 (p. 3)
A. 18   B. 26   C. 14   D. 39

Addition 3 (p. 3)
A. 44   B. 18   C. 12   D. 42

Addition 4 (p. 3)
A. 9   B. 5   C. 20   D. 7

Addition 5 (p. 3)
A. 7   B. 17   C. 19   D. 5

Addition 6 (p. 4)
17 + ___ = 32   Answer: 15

Addition 7 (p. 4)
27

Addition 8 (p. 4)
650

Addition 9 (p. 4)
50

Addition 10 (p. 4)
A. 13   B. 252

Addition 11 (p. 5)
A. 11   B. 9   C. 14   D. 9

Addition 12 (p. 5)
A. $18   B. $26   C. $14   D. $39

Addition 13 (p. 5)
A. 0.44   B. 0.18   C. 0.12   D. 0.42

Addition 14 (p. 5)
A. 8   B. 6   C. 19   D. 5

Addition 15 (p. 5)
A. 6   B. 20   C. 19   D. 16

Subtraction 1 (p. 6)
A. 3   B. 7   C. 4   D. 18

Subtraction 2 (p. 6)
A. 52   B. 4   C. 82   D. 42

Subtraction 3 (p. 6)
A. 19   B. 106   C. 48   D. 95

Subtraction 4 (p. 6)
A. 3   B. 3   C. 24   D. 51

Subtraction 5 (p. 6)
A. 11   B. 29   C. 11   D. 67

Subtraction 6 (p. 7)
A. 10   B. 11   C. 46   D. 73

Subtraction 7 (p. 7)
A. $52   B. $44   C. $82   D. $39

Subtraction 8 (p. 7)
A. 1.29   B. 1.66   C. 0.28   D. 1.40

Subtraction 9 (p. 7)
A. 2   B. 14   C. 43   D. 43

Subtraction 10 (p. 7)
A. 4   B. 26   C. 21   D. 76

Multiplication 1 (p. 8)
A. 10   B. 3   C. 4   D. 9

Multiplication 2 (p. 8)
A. 4   B. 4   C. 7   D. 4

Multiplication 3 (p. 8)
A. 2   B. 4   C. 3   D. 3

Multiplication 4 (p. 8)
A. 2   B. 3   C. 1   D. 2

Multiplication 5 (p. 8)
A. 12   B. 6   C. 3   D. 26

Multiplication 6 (p. 9)
A. 5   B. 4   C. 7   D. 6

Multiplication 7 (p. 9)
A. 4   B. 3   C. 7   D. 6

Multiplication 8 (p. 9)
A. 2   B. 4   C. 3   D. 3

Multiplication 9 (p. 9)
A. 10   B. 4   C. 9   D. 7

Multiplication 10 (p. 9)
A. 7   B. $9

Arrays 1 (p. 10)
11 x 3 = 33 and 3 x 11 = 33

Arrays 2 (p. 10)
A. 15   B. 36   C. 24   D. 15

Arrays 3 (p. 10)
A. 4   8 = 32 and 8   4 = 32
B. 7   5 = 35 and 5   7 = 35

Arrays 4 (p. 10)
A. 135   B. 192

Arrays 5 (p. 10)
156

Division 1 (p. 11)
A. 6   B. 48   C. 11   D. 35

Division 2 (p. 11)
A. 4   B. $28 C. 8   D. $144

Division 3 (p. 11)
A. 6   B. 62   C. 9   D. 65

Division 4 (p. 11)
A. 10   B. 200 C. 100 D. 45,000

Division 5 (p. 11)
A. 92 ÷ 23 = 4   B. 56 ÷ 7 = 8

Division 6 (p. 12)
A. 6   B. 48   C. 11   D. 35

Division 7 (p. 12)
A. 5   B. $42 C. 9   D. $132

Division 8 (p. 12)
A. 6   B. 58   C. 9   D. 64

Division 9 (p. 12)
A. 10   B. 100 C. 1,000 D. 63,000

Division 10 (p. 12)
A. 56   B. 60

Mixed Operations: Math Stories 1 (p. 13)
She baked 23 cookies.

Mixed Operations: Math Stories 2 (p. 13)
A. $280   B. $3.15

Mixed Operations: Math Stories 3 (p. 13)
A. 1 stack of 12, 2 stacks of 6, 3 stacks of 4, 4 stacks of 3, 6 stacks of 2, 12 stacks of 1
B. 5

Mixed Operations: Math Stories 4 (p. 13)
A. She has 2 tens and 13 ones.
B. He has 2 ones.

Mixed Operations: Math Stories 5 (p. 13)
A. $84   B. 45 carrots

Decimals and Fractions 1 (p. 14)
A. $\frac{3}{4}$ B. $\frac{19}{20}$ C. $\frac{1}{5}$ D. $\frac{17}{50}$
E. $\frac{1}{100}$ F. $7\frac{7}{50}$

Decimals and Fractions 2 (p. 14)
A. 0.8   B. 0.9   C. 0.07   D. 0.875
E. 0.5   F. 5.6

Decimals and Fractions 3 (p. 14)
A. $17\frac{1}{4}$ B. $\frac{29}{40}$ C. $1\frac{5}{27}$ D. $\frac{5}{14}$

Decimals and Fractions 4 (p. 14)
A. $\frac{1}{2}$ B. 3   C. 0.18   D. 5

Decimals and Fractions 5 (p. 14)
A. $\frac{3}{4}$ B. 4   C. $30\frac{1}{4}$ D. 2.6

Order of Operations 1 (p. 15)
A. 22   B. 14   C. 15   D. 50

Order of Operations 2 (p. 15)
A. 31   B. 35   C. -25   D. -18

Order of Operations 3 (p. 15)
A. $79 B. $18

Order of Operations 4 (p. 15)
A. 56 B. 5 C. 24 D. -0.66

Order of Operations 5 (p. 15)
A. 102 B. 6 C. 26 D. 113

Order of Operations 6 (p. 16)
A. 8 B. 4 C. 3

Order of Operations 7 (p. 16)
A. 2 B. 6 C. 9

Order of Operations 8 (p. 16)
A. 5 B. 10 C. 4

Order of Operations 9 (p. 16)
A. Answers will vary. An example would be: 2; 3
B. Answers will vary. An example would be: 5; 4
C. Answers will vary. An example would be: 6; 7

Order of Operations 10 (p. 16)
A. 8 B. 9 C. 10 D. 0

Positive and Negative Numbers 1 (p. 17)
A. 11° B. 9°

Positive and Negative Numbers 2 (p. 17)
A. -23° B. -46°

Positive and Negative Numbers 3 (p. 17)
A. 30° B. -21°

Positive and Negative Numbers 4 (p. 17)
$18.50

Positive and Negative Numbers 5 (p. 17)

Amount Due	Amount Paid	Balance	20% Interest	New Balance
$400.00	$20.00	$380.00	$6.33	$386.33
$386.33	$20.00	$366.33	$6.11	$372.44
$372.44	$20.00	$352.44	$5.87	$358.31
$358.31	$20.00	$338.31	$5.64	$343.95
$343.95	$20.00	$323.95	$5.40	$329.35
$329.35	$20.00	$309.35	$5.16	$314.51

Positive and Negative Numbers 6 (p. 18)
A. -3 + -1 + -5 = -9 B. (-5 -1) + -3 = +2
C. (-5 -3) + -1 = +14 D. (-5 + -3) ÷ -1 = +8

Positive and Negative Numbers 7 (p. 18)
A. (-2 + -6) ÷ -4 = +2
B. (-4 -6) + -2 = +22
C. (-2 -4) + -6 = +2
D. -6 + -2 + -4 = -12

Positive and Negative Numbers 8 (p. 18)
A. -5 + -6 + -7 = -18
B. (-7 -6) + -5 = +37
C. (-5 -6) + -7 = +23
D. (-5 -6) ÷ -7 = -4 R2

Positive and Negative Numbers 9 (p. 18)
A. (-3 + -1) -5 = +20
B. -3 + (-5 ÷ -1) = +2
C. (-5 + -1) -3 = +18
D. (-3 -5) ÷ -1 = -15

Positive and Negative Numbers 10 (p. 18)
A. (-6 -5) ÷ -4 = -7 R2
B. (-4 -6) ÷ -5 = -4 R4
C. -4 + -5 + -6 = -15
D. -6 (-5 + -4) = +54

Exponents 1 (p. 19)
A. 2 2 2 2
B. 9 9 9 9 9 9
C. 7 7 7
D. $y \cdot y \cdot y \cdot y \cdot y \cdot y \cdot y \cdot y \cdot y$

Exponents 2 (p. 19)
A. 27 B. 16 C. 32 D. 125

Exponents 3 (p. 19)
A. 3^3 B. 10^6 C. d^3 D. $m^2 + p^2$

Exponents 4 (p. 19)
A. 16 B. 26 C. 24 D. 33

Exponents 5 (p. 19)
A. 6^2 B. 9^2 (or 3^4) C. 4^2 (or 2^4) D. 5^2

Multi-Step Math Stories 1 (p. 20)
A. $9,600 B. $325

Multi-Step Math Stories 2 (p. 20)
The youngest paid $20; the others paid $30 each.

Multi-Step Math Stories 3 (p. 20)
A. 2   B. 1

Multi-Step Math Stories 4 (p. 20)
A. $204   B. $82.50

Operations Signs 1 (p. 21)
A. +   B. ÷   C.   D. −

Operations Signs 2 (p. 21)
A.   B. +   C. −   D. +

Operations Signs 3 (p. 21)
A. +   B. ÷   C.   D. +, +

Operations Signs 4 (p. 21)
A. >   B. <   C. >   D. =

Operations Signs 5 (p. 21)
A. =   B. >   C. =   D. >
E. ≥   F. <

Mixed Operations 1 (p. 22)
Missing: 18

Mixed Operations 2 (p. 22)
Missing: 54

Mixed Operations 3 (p. 22)
Missing: 230

Mixed Operations 4 (p. 22)
Missing: ; ; −; ÷

Mixed Operations 5 (p. 22)
Missing: 1.5

Describing Number Patterns 1 (p. 23)
35: $n + 7$

Describing Number Patterns 2 (p. 23)
A. 32; 128: n 2
B. 77; 66; 55; 44: $n - 11$

Describing Number Patterns 3 (p. 23)
A. 31: n 2 + 1
B. 16: $n \div 2$

Describing Number Patterns 4 (p. 23)
n cats have 2 times n ears; $2n$

Describing Number Patterns 5 (p. 23)
$n + 2$

Drawing a Picture or Diagram to Find a Pattern 1 (p. 24)
20 ducklings

Drawing a Picture or Diagram to Find a Pattern 2 (p. 24)
10 cans

Drawing a Picture or Diagram to Find a Pattern 3 (p. 24)
Students should draw a 5 by 5 array of diamonds.

Drawing a Picture or Diagram to Find a Pattern 4 (p. 24)
Students should continue the pattern with drawings of 10 and 15 apples.

Drawing a Picture or Diagram to Find a Pattern 5 (p. 24)
Items drawn should show 3, 6, 9, 12, and 15 items.

Using Tables to Find Patterns 1 (p. 25)
At 10 P.M., it was -11°.

Using Tables to Find Patterns 2 (p. 25)
14 were red.

Using Tables to Find Patterns 3 (p. 25)
48 people rode the "red eye."

Using Tables to Find Patterns 4 (p. 25)
She spent 4 hours reading.

Using Tables to Find Patterns 5 (p. 25)
Grace has 42 rock CDs, 14 country CDs, and 21 jazz CDs.

Math Stories With Patterns 1 (p. 26)
A. 72% B. 96%

Math Stories With Patterns 2 (p. 26)
A. 34 minutes B. 106 minutes

Math Stories With Patterns 3 (p. 26)
A. $13.12 B. $10.63

Math Stories With Patterns 4 (p. 26)
She will need to proofread 6 times.

Math Stories With Patterns 5 (p. 26)
There were 14 dogs and 8 owners.

Values of Variables 1 (p. 27)
A. 52 B. 60 C. 53 D. 99

Values of Variables 2 (p. 27)
A. 57 B. 0 C. -13 D. 60

Values of Variables 3 (p. 27)
A. -40 B. 12 C. -84 D. -36

Values of Variables 4 (p. 27)
A. b 0.75 B. $12.75

Values of Variables 5 (p. 27)
A. $2d + \$0.75m$ B. $16.75

Balancing Equations 1 (p. 28)
A. 9 B. 3 C. 6 + 12

Balancing Equations 2 (p. 28)
A. 5 B. 5 C. 31 − 8

Balancing Equations 3 (p. 28)
A. Answer can be any number.
B. 4 C. z 3 0.5 6

Balancing Equations 4 (p. 28)
A. 7 B. 4 C. 20 ÷ 1

Balancing Equations 5 (p. 28)
A. 9 − 4 B. 84; 84 − 9
C. $y ÷ 11$ 4

Balancing Equations 6 (p. 29)
A. subtract B. subtract
C. add D. add

Balancing Equations 7 (p. 29)
A. multiply B. divide
C. subtract D. multiply

Balancing Equations 8 (p. 29)
A. 702 B. $\frac{1}{2}$

Balancing Equations 9 (p. 29)
A. divide B. multiply
C. add D. subtract

Balancing Equations 10 (p. 29)
A. 6,491 B. 12

Isolating Variables 1 (p. 30)
A. 4 B. 74 C. 28

Isolating Variables 2 (p. 30)
A. 23 B. 92 C. 6

Isolating Variables 3 (p. 30)
A. 3 B. 4 C. 5

Isolating Variables 4 (p. 30)
A. 12 B. 21 C. 40

Isolating Variables 5 (p. 30)
A. 3 B. 1 C. 3

Isolating Variables 6 (p. 31)
A. 28 B. 729 C. 2 D. 83

Isolating Variables 7 (p. 31)
A. 5 B. 7 C. 183 D. 8

Isolating Variables 8 (p. 31)
A. 4 B. 288 C. 45 D. 63

Isolating Variables 9 (p. 31)
A. 4 B. 5 C. 217 D. 3

Isolating Variables 10 (p. 31)
A. $p ÷ 12 = 10$; $p = 120$ B. 390 inches
C. 39 inches

Step-by Step 1 (p. 32)
$n + \$1,582 = \$5,387$ $n = \$5,387 − \$1,582$
$n = \$3,805$

Step-by-Step 2 (p. 32)
$h + 128 = 374$ $h = 374 - 128$
$h = 246$

Step-by-Step 3 (p. 32)
$m - \$4.36 = \$3.92$ $m = \$3.92 + \$4.36$
$m = \$8.28$

Step-by-Step 4 (p. 32)
$8p = 48$ $p = 48 \div 8$
$p = 6$

Step-by-Step 5 (p. 32)
$7 + 9 + j = 19$ $j = 19 - 16$
$j = 3$

Variables in Measurement 1 (p. 33)
A. 3　b or $3b$　　B. 16　z or $16z$

Variables in Measurement 2 (p. 33)
A. 5,280　c or $5,280c$　B. $d \div 36$

Variables in Measurement 3 (p. 33)
A. 2　e or $2e$　　B. $f \div 4$

Variables in Measurement 4 (p. 33)
A. g　60 or $60g$
B. h　24　60 or $1,440h$

Variables in Measurement 5 (p. 33)
A. 7　j or $7j$　　B. $k \div 7$

Variables in Formulas 1 (p. 34)
A. $A = 5$　7; 35 sq. ft.
B. $A = 9$　11; 99 sq. mm

Variables in Formulas 2 (p. 34)
A. $A = \frac{1}{2}(6)(7)$; 21 sq. ft.
B. $A = \frac{1}{2}(10)(9)$; 45 sq. in.

Variables in Formulas 3 (p. 34)
A. $V = 9$　9　9; 729 cu. in.
B. $V = 4$　7　8; 224 cu. ft.
C. $V = 4$　8　7; 224 cu. mm
D. $V = 6$　2　25; 300 cu. cm

Variables in Formulas 4 (p. 34)
A. area, length, width
B. The area of a triangle equals $\frac{1}{2}$ its base times its height.
C. The volume of a rectangular prism equals its length times its width times its height.

Variables in Formulas 5 (p. 34)
A. 700 sq. ft.　B. 16 sq. in.　C. 343 cu. in.

Variables in Formulas 6 (p. 35)
A. $d = 55$　4; 220 miles
B. $r = 123 \div 3$; 41 miles per hour
C. $r = 12 \div 3$; 4 miles per hour

Variables in Formulas 7 (p. 35)
A. 21.4 miles per hour　　B. 225 feet
C. 5 yards per second

Variables in Formulas 8 (p. 35)
A. $18 \div 2.5 = t$; 7.2 hours
B. $867 \div 3 = r$; 289 miles per hour

Variables in Formulas 9 (p. 35)
A. 420 feet　　B. 15 seconds

Multi-Step Operations With Variables 1 (p. 36)
6 were 11, 15 were 12, and 9 were 13.

Multi-Step Operations With Variables 2 (p. 36)
There were 45 clownfish, 15 angelfish, 160 neon tetras, and 80 zebra fish.

Multi-Step Operations With Variables 3 (p. 36)
A. 432 trees　　B. 144 cedar

Multi-Step Operations With Variables 4 (p. 36)
Since the hare had covered 348 feet by the time the tortoise covered 12 feet, the hare was 336 feet ahead.

Multi-Step Operations With Variables 5 (p. 36)
A. 6 bouquets
B. 2 more full bouquets with 2 flowers left

Multi-Step Operations With Variables 6 (p. 37)
He has 6 green hats and 3 red hats.

Multi-Step Operations With Variables 7 (p. 37)
Paul rode 30 miles, and Pam rode 10 miles.

Multi-Step Operations With Variables 8 (p. 37)
She has 21 pepper plants, 7 tomato plants, and 28 basil plants.

Multi-Step Operations With Variables 9 (p. 37)
Robin and Lark each saw 240 birds; Jay saw 120 birds.

Multi-Step Operations With Variables 10 (p. 37)
There were 20 pieces of shrimp, 20 pieces of pepperoni, and 80 chunks of pineapple.

Value of Variables Using Clues 1 (p. 38)
The lowest possible value of $t = 105$.

Value of Variables Using Clues 2 (p. 38)
The highest possible value of $b = 88$.

Value of Variables Using Clues 3 (p. 38)
The only possible value of $w = 51$.

Value of Variables Using Clues 4 (p. 38)
Students should answer two of these three possible values for n: 15; 45; 75.

Value of Variables Using Clues 5 (p. 38)
The only possible value of $c = 49$.

Equations With Two Variables 1 (p. 39)
A. $y = 35$ B. $y = 51$
C. $y = 7$ D. $y = 4$

Equations With Two Variables 2 (p. 39)
A. $g = 7\frac{1}{4}$ B. $g = 7$
C. $g = 2$ D. $g = 17\frac{1}{4}$

Equations With Two Variables 3 (p. 39)
A. 12   B. 2   C. 32   D. 33

Equations With Two Variables 4 (p. 39)
A. $r + t = 73$ or $t + r = 73$
B. $r - t = 128$ or $t - r = 128$

Equations With Two Variables 5 (p. 39)
A. $v \div w = 8$ or $w \div v = 8$
B. $84 \quad v = w$ or $84 \quad w = v$